Hinduism for Beginners

Guide to Understanding Hinduism and the Hindu
Religion, Beliefs, Customs, Rituals, Gods, Mantras
and Converting to Hinduism

By

Shalu Sharma

Other books by Shalu Sharma -
http://www.amazon.com/author/shalusharma

Hinduism For Kids: Beliefs And Practices
Hinduism Made Easy: Hindu Religion, Philosophy and Concepts
Religions of the World for Kids
Buddhism Made Easy: Buddhism for Beginners and Busy People
Mother Teresa of Calcutta: Finding God Helping Others: Life of Mother Teresa

ISBN-13: 978-1523472826
ISBN-10: 1523472820

Table of Contents

Introduction to Hinduism

Hinduism is the third most popular religion in the world and has more than 750 million followers. Hinduism is predominately practiced in the country of India, which is where it originated back in ancient times. Today more than 80% of the Indian population identify themselves as Hindu. With a country of 1.3 billion people, this means about 1 billion Indian residents are Hindus. This makes Hinduism a substantial part of Indian culture and many of the customs and traditions of the religion are integrated into India's everyday society. For example, the cow is respected and honored by Hindus because they are seen as a symbol of life. You will find cows simply roaming the streets of India's towns and cities because the nation's culture is accepting towards cows. This culture is based on a religious principle and since India has one billion people who are Hindu, the religion itself has been adapted into the standards of Indian society. Now there are many Indian states that will criminally prosecute you for killing cows or going against other Hindu traditions. However, many of the Hindu traditions involve standard beliefs that are shared around the world such as don't kill, steal or assault anyone.

Historians and scholars tend to debate when Hinduism first got started, but the archaeological evidence suggests it began in India sometime around 2,000 B.C. No other religion that exists today is as old as Hinduism. The teachings of the religion have been passed down through the teachings of prophets and ancient scriptures written in Sanskrit. The Vedas is the largest collection of scriptures that was compiled back in 1,500 B.C., but most historians believe the scriptures that make up the Vedas were written much earlier. The Vedic Sanskrit is by far the oldest Sanskrit literature in existence and contains the oldest Hindu scriptures. The Vedas is like the Holy Bible of Hinduism and it is the book that every Hindu looks upon for spiritual guidance and religious education. On a side note, the Vedas were completed 1,000 years before the Christian Holy Bible was even written. This proves that Hinduism is much older than Christianity or Catholicism.

As you learn about Hinduism, you will find that it is a very unique religion. Unlike most religions, there is no declared founder of Hinduism. The religion is simply made up of a collection of beliefs and writings that were put together, which eventually became the Vedas. There is no official Hindu church or gathering where Hindus go every week to pray. Hindus simply pray at temples whenever they want to gather spiritual strength or when they want to pray. They will even pray to the Gods of Hinduism, such as Ganesha, Parvati, Saraswati, Shiva, Krishna and the main God "Brahman" (not the God of creation Brahma or to be confused with Brahmin). This is the God that all the other Gods are made from. In fact, all life on Earth is part of Brahman. As you read through this book, you will learn exactly why Brahman is so worshipped by Hindus and why accepting his power will bring them closer to enlightenment.

Important Beliefs in Hinduism

A true Hindu keeps their faith and religious beliefs with them 24 hours per day. They wake up each morning, pray and read mantras from the Vedas. There is nothing more important to Hindus than practicing their religious beliefs in their everyday lives. They believe Hinduism is a religion of love because all Hindus are supposed to be spiritually connected into one entity, according to the laws of dharma and karma (deeds). That is why when someone dies they are not lost forever. They just take the form of a new body within the one spiritual body that all Hindus are a part of. If Hindus are good throughout their multiple lives and follow all the rules and traditions of Hinduism then their soul will eventually end up in a total state of enlightenment with the one true God called Brahman.

Karma is the Hindu belief that a person's destiny is determined by their actions while they are alive. If a person lives a life of righteousness then they will live an even better life when they are reborn. But if a person lives a bad life then they will be reborn into a worse life. Obviously, Hindus want to live their lives righteously so they can keep their karma good and strong. If their karma remains good long enough through the cycle of rebirth then they will attain Moksha, which is absolute spiritual knowledge and the freedom to move beyond the cycle of rebirth towards enlightenment. This enlightenment has to do with having your individual soul become part of Brahman's universal soul. This is an important goal to Hindus.

For thousands of years, Hindus have studied the Vedas written in the Sanskrit language. There are four Vedas namely the Rigveda, the Yajurveda, the Samaveda and the Atharvaveda. These are ancient scriptures and naturally the first scriptures to come out of Hinduism. These books are said to contain the words and song of God. However, they don't refer to him as "God" like people in other religions do. They simply call him the Supreme Being or the Creator, which is believed to exist inside all life on Earth. But this being is not subject to the limitations of the physical world or the physical human appearance. He is not a God that is represented as a human figure or an old man in the sky. You could say that everything is a representation of the Supreme Being. Now despite the differences between Hinduism and other religions, Hindus still have a genuine respect for people of all religions and faiths. In fact, Hindus are not one to say that Hinduism or any other religion is the only religion that teaches the truth about God and the way towards salvation. They believe that the paths to salvation in every religion are part of the Supreme Being's pure love and light. This means other religions deserve understanding and tolerance as well.

In Hinduism, the shared belief is that there is the existence of three worlds; casual, astral and physical. They also believe the universe goes through infinite cycles of formation, termination and preservation. Most people outside of Hinduism are only familiar with the physical world and not the casual and astral worlds. But what these people don't realize is that they already exist in these three worlds. The physical world is simply the world where everybody lives. It is the world you are in right now and the world where your physical body lies. The astral world is where your emotional body resides, which is separate from the physical world. All of the feelings you conjure up in your lifetime exist in the astral world. As for the casual world, this is the place where your deepest thoughts and ideas are. These three worlds are talked about in the Bhagavad Gita, which is a 700 verse epic that was written in Sanskrit back in 300 B.C. This book contains a story written as a poem and its subtext provides a powerful philosophical message to Hindus in regards to the teachings of Hinduism. That is why this book is highly regarded and read frequently by its followers.

Temples and shrines are very common in Hinduism. They are places where Hindus go to worship the divine beings that exist in our world and the other worlds that we cannot see. There are also rituals and sacraments that take place in them. Hindus will practically devote themselves entirely to the Gods and devas of all these worlds. Remember there are multiple Gods that exist, which are all part of the overall creator of the world; Brahman. This is the God that is part of all life on Earth. Besides wanting good karma, another big reason why Hindus want to do good deeds for others is because they believe all life is sacred and that people are to be loved. This belief in sacred life comes from the other belief that Brahman is part of all life. So if they were to injure someone then it would really be an attack on their greatest God, which is something they obviously would not want to do.

Of course, Hindus are still human beings and they cannot always trust themselves to act decently all the time. That is why Hindus have developed special spiritual exercises which they believe calms their spirit and allows them to be good towards others. One popular exercise is called yoga. It is a great way to physically and mentally discipline oneself in order to achieve tranquility and absolute purification of the soul. That way it will reduce your chances of being angry and committing acts of violence against other people. By refraining from these actions it will help your karma, which is one of the main goals of Hindus. The most important goal is to achieve Moksha. The way to achieve this is by increasing your good karma, which is why karma and Moksha typically intertwine with each other. The other two important goals are to practice Dharma and Artha. Dharma is basically a code that Hindus study which teach them how to live their lives properly. It basically says they should respect their elders and if you are a son then you must get married. As for Artha, this represents people's pursuit of wealth and knowledge through legal means. Kama (different from karma) is about fulfilling ones worldly desires. This could be in the form of a job, money and wealth, sex etc without harming others. Hindus are happy when they have achieved Artha, Dharma, Kama and Moksha.

Maya is another concept in Hinduism where everything is an illusion. Under the influence of "maya" the soul identifies itself with the body and ignorance begins to creep in and gets entangled in pursuing material life. Maya literally means "that which is not there". For instance, a person can mistake a rope for a snake but clearly it's not a snake. One who realizes that body and soul are different becomes free from maya. Those who are spiritually inclined or those who are able to sense the truth, the reality of God, discard their ego - they become free from the clutches of maya.

Important Hindu Customs and Rituals

Much of the religious lives of the Hindus are spent focused on the devotion of Brahman or the Supreme Being (Brahman) or worshiping one person God (Krishna, Shiva, Ganesha, Hanuman etc). This is done in the form of numerous religious rituals and practices. Here are a few important ones. Not many people will observe them all.

Namaste (also Pranam)

This is a salutation used for greeting others. This is done by folding both palms together and prostrating or bowing slightly towards to the person who you are greeting and saying "Namaste". The same method is applied when worshipping or prayers (no need to say "Namaste"). That is why you see Hindus standing in front of their Gods with folded hands.

Puja (Pooja or Poojah)

The puja is way of showing reverence to any one particular God. This is done by sitting in front of idol of image and offering flowers, ghee, fruits, carrying a fire sacrifice etc and singing devotional songs called bhajans. It can be done at home or at a temple.

Havan or Homa (Fire sacrifice)

This forms part of the puja. One way to offer something to the Gods is through the fire. A fire alter is made and offerings in the form of ghee (butter, sandal wood, cow dung, coconut etc are added. Havan is carried out for good health, self confidence, to ward off evil spirits, overcome obstacles, wealth, attain Moksha, blessings from the Gods, getting rid of evil influences, renunciation etc. You can do this yourself or you can take the help of a pundit (priest) to do a havan.

Ayurveda

Ayurveda (Ayurvedic medicine) is very popular in India. It's an ancient system of natural healing. It is often used as part of general wellbeing along with Western medicine. Ayurvedic practitioners use the 5 senses and use 8 ways to diagnose illness, called Mootra (urine), Shabda (speech), Sparsha (touch), Mala (stool), Nadi (pulse), Jihva (tongue), Druk (vision), and Aakruti (appearance).

Sadhus, Gurus and Pandits

Many Hindus utilize the services of Sadhus, Gurus and Pandits. Sandhus are holy men who have renounced the world and are on a spiritual path. Gurus are like teachers or guides who impart knowledge on a particular topic. Pandits are priests; most of them belong to the Brahmin caste (the priestly caste).

The 4 Ashramas of life

According to Hinduism a person has 4 stages of life. The 4 Asramas are: Brahmacharya (student), Grihastha (householder), Vanaprastha (retired) and Sannyasa (renunciation).

Brahmacharya Ashrama or the first stage as a bachelor and acquiring knowledge.

Grihastha Ashrama or the second stage as someone who is married and looks after the family.

Vanaprastha Ashrama or the hermit stage where one is to renounce sex and become a hermit.

Sannyasa Ashrama as a wandering ascetic. In this stage the person is totally devoted to God and committed to attaining moksha.

Purification

In Hinduism, taking a daily bath is an important ritual. Early morning at about 4 is considered as most auspicious. It is well established that a Hindu when performing any "puja" or before going to a temple should take a shower. Many Hindus take a dip in the holy Ganges River to remove impurities from the soul while chanting mantras to enhance the cleansing process. During the Kumbh Mela festival millions of Hindus take a dip in the River Ganges. Ordinary Hindus take a shower and then offer their prayers in front of an idol/image before carrying out other worldly duties.

Vegetarianism

Many Hindus are vegetarians. They are of the view that all living things have a soul and it is not right to kill them even for food. Those who do eat meat will not consume it during festivals.

Marriages

Marriages are considered to be made in heaven. Hindus believe the same people will get married in each life. Most marriages are arranged. There is a big ceremony to celebrate weddings. Married women wear mangalsutras in their neck, apply vermillion on their front head, a bindi on their forehead and wear bangles and toe rings to indicate that they are married.

Respect to elders

Showing respect to elders is an important aspect of Hindu culture. The younger generation presupposed to touch the feet of their elders. They are ones to offer salutations (Namaste) first upon meeting.

Death

Death is not seen as the end of life but as a new beginning according to the deeds or karma they have committed. The soul is immortal but the body is subjected to ever ending cycle of birth and rebirth till the soul reaches perfection and attains Moksha. Reincarnation is an important aspect in Hinduism hence rituals after death of an individual are carried out so that the departed soul can be at peace.

The caste system

The caste system was not always part of the Hindu religion but in the 6th century it became very rigid. There are 4 varnas (Sanskrit word mentioned in the Rig Veda) according to social status namely the Brahmins (the priestly class- not to be confused with "Brahman"), Kshatriyas (the warrior and ruling class), Vaishyas (business class) and the Sudras (the labourers and service providers). Although practice of the caste system is still there in India but discrimination against any castes are not allowed and is a crime in India.

Aarti

A ritual that forms part of a puja. Aartis comprise of a plate made of silver, bronze or copper with a small fire made of ghee or oil. Hindus believe that any offerings to the Gods can be done though the fire. After the ceremonies and puja are over, devotees take the blessing by placing their hand close to the fire and then touching their forehead.

Introduction to Gods and Goddesses in Hinduism

There are 3 major traditions in Hinduism namely Shaivism, Vaishnavism and Shaktism which consider Shiva, Vishnu and Shakti as their main God respectively. Other deities are considered as reincarnations to the world whenever the devotees required them.

Let's take a look at some of the popular Gods and Goddesses in Hinduism.

Brahma (not Brahman the Supreme Being) – He is considered as the creator of the universe.

Vishnu - Vishnu is the preserver of the universe. Lord Rama and Krishna are his incarnations.

Shiva – One of the major Gods in Hinduism. Shiva is the destroyer or the Transformer.

Ganesha – The Elephant God and is the one who removes obstacles.

Hanuman – The Monkey God and a prominent character in the Epic Ramayana.

Rama – The seventh Avatar of Lord Vishnu. He is considered as the ideal being for a man to follow.

Krishna – He is the eighth Avatar of Lord Vishnu and one of the most popular Gods in Hinduism.

Durga –Durga is one of the most revered Goddesses in Hinduism. She is known as Devi and Shakti. She is the principal cause of creation, preservation and annihilation.

Parvati – Parvati is the wife of Shiva. She is worshipped as the Goddess of divine strength and power.

Saraswati – She is the Goddess of knowledge, education and creativity.

Lakshmi- She is the Goddess of wealth and prosperity. She is particularly worshipped on the festival of Diwali.

Sita - Sita is the wife of Lord Ram and the ideal being for a woman to follow.

Gayatri – She is the feminine form of Gayatra and worshipped as a Goddess.

Bhagavad Gita

If you want to learn more about Hinduism then you should definitely read the Bhagavad Gita. The Bhagavad Gita is a Hindu scripture written in Sanskrit back in 300 B.C. It is part of the Hindu epic entitled "Mahabharata," which is one of the two most popular ancient Indian epics written in Sanskrit. In English, Bhagavad Gita means "Song of the Lord." Bhagavad is translated into "God" and Gita is translated into "song." However, this scripture does not contain lyrics to any literal song. Instead the story within the scripture is told as a poem. The reason why it is called a song is because the words of the poem rhyme with each other. To a Hindu reading these words consecutively, it will start to sound like a song to them whether they are reading it to themselves or out loud. Gita is admired by Hindus for its devotional and philosophical subtext. It is an example of how they should fulfill their duties in order to find Dharma. More importantly, the Gita helps Hindus obtain spiritual wisdom through the stories that are told in its scripture. This practice has been done for thousands of years ever since the Gita was first written.

The epic is a narrative that tells the story of the Kurukshetra War and the battle between Pandava and Kaurava princes. A lot of the narrative dialogue in this scripture actually takes place between the Pandava Prince named Arjuna and the God who is guiding him named Krishna. Lord Krishna is also the God that first spoke the words contained in the Gita. These words were spoken in Kurukshetra, which is a town that is now considered to be holy land because of its history with Krishna speaking the words of the Gita there. It is also holy because the true Creator, Lord Brahma, told King Kuru that anyone who performs penance on this land will get to spend their afterlife in the heavenly planets instead of being reincarnated back on Earth. This motivates millions of Hindus to travel to Kurukshetra every year to perform their own penance in order to get a shot at this great fate.

There are 700 verses contained in Sanskrit of the Bhagavad Gita and there are 32 syllables per verse. There verses were divided into 18 chapters and those chapters were divided into 3 sections; Karma Yoga, Bhakti Yoga and Jnana Yoga. Karma Yoga represents action, Bhakti Yoga represents devotion and Jnana Yoga represents knowledge. So when Hindus are reading this "song of the Lord," the overall message they are getting is in regard to the action they must take, the devotion to make and the knowledge needed to succeed. Now this message may apply to different people in different ways, but the action, knowledge and devotion people make to Hinduism will be the same.

The Bhagavad Gita has been translated hundreds of times over the last 2,000 years since it was written. The first English translation of the Gita came out in 1785. Then in the 19th century it was translated into Greek, Spanish, French, Latin and German. Today you can find the content of the Gita in virtually any language and it is accessible for free on the internet.

You can learn more about the Bhagavad Gita in this book by Swami Vivekananda - Lectures on the Bhagavad Gita (Annotated Edition - ISBN-10: 1515186792) or The Song Celestial or Bhagavad-Gita by Sir Edwin Arnold - ISBN-10: 1514733269.

Hindu Festivals

India is a big country. It's famous for its billion people, numerous languages, cows, call centers, curry and, of course, festivals. The festivals are an Indian specialty. Every second day someone in the same region of the country is celebrating something. Though it's not possible to get them all listed, we will however take a brief overview of the festivals in India.

Pan Indian festivals

These are festivals that are celebrated throughout India and to some extent in the neighboring countries too.

Diwali

It wouldn't be an exaggeration to call Diwali the most important festival of the Indian subcontinent. It offers one of the few occasions when, irrespective of their religion, ethnicity, caste or color, people join each other in celebrations. Each has its own historic reason to celebrate. The Hindus celebrate to commemorate the mythical king Rama's return to his kingdom of Ayodhya. It falls in late autumn or early winter each year.

Holi

Historically it was an agricultural festival to celebrate the arrival of spring. With time, however, it has changed. There is now elaborate mythology associated with Holi. Despite this, Holi is widely regarded as a festival when people can throw away traditional social norms and indulge in merrymaking. There are pujas (prayers) held in several parts of the country. However, generally speaking, it's more about sensual pleasure than any gods or goddesses.

Dussehra

This is the worship of Goddess Durga hence also called Durga Puja. It marks the destruction of evil and the victory of good. Durga Puja is celebrated every year from the sixth to tenth day of bright lunar fortnight.

Regional festivals

These festivals hold great significance and are celebrated with great fanfare, but only in a particular region.

Snake boat race, Kerala

Held during the wet Monsoon season, the snake boat race festival is very a popular festival in the South Indian state of Kerala. Snake boats are unusually long (more than 100 feet) canoes in which more than 100 rowers can sit. Teams of rowers compete against each other during the festival season which culminates in Onam (the most popular festival in Kerala).

Festivals for women

These are the days when only ladies can have fun!

Karva chauth

This festival is popular among married North Indian women who stay without food or water for a day and pray for the longevity and safety for their husbands.

Rakhi

On this day, sisters tie a piece of thread on their brothers' arms for their safety and longevity. In return, the brothers promise to protect their sisters forever and offer them gifts.

Newly created festivals

There are several festivals that have come into being only in the past few decades. Mango Festival (Uttar Pradesh), Elephant festival (Kerala), Garden festival (Delhi) and numerous others are recent (mainly government) creations to economically support local culture by making them attractive to tourists.

The Hindu mind, like the Hindu faith, has a facility for accepting, semi-assimilating, and finally absorbing, all of religious belief and conviction that may come into contact with it.

Non-Hindu festivals popular in India

Gurupurab, Punjab

Gurupurabs are days when Sikh gurus were born or died. These days have a historic significance to both Hindus and Sikhs in Punjab. They are very popular in the tiny northern state where devotees organise langar (free kitchen) and chhabeel (free drinks) on roads and in gurudwaras.

Chhath, Celebrated mainly in Bihar and neighbouring states of Jharakhand, Uttar Pradesh and neighbouring country Nepal. Chhath is a big occasion to thank the sun god for sustaining life on earth. The festivities continue for four days, of which the third day, of Chhath, is the most important. There are elaborate rituals and prayers associated with the festival.

Eid-ul-Fitr and Eid-ul-Adha

These are two popular festivals in the states of Jammu and Kashmir and parts of Andhra Prades, Uttar Pradesh and Bihar. Eid-ul-Fitr is the day of festivities after a long month of fasting (Ramazan). Eid-ul -Adha is the day when people commemorate Abraham's sacrifice of his son Ishmael.

Guru Nanak Jayanti

Guru Nanak was the first Guru of the Sikhs and the founder of Sikhism. Guru Nanak Jayanti is celebrated on his birthday.

Muharram

The festival of Muharram is festival of the Shia Muslims. It is the first month of the Islamic calendar. Many Hindus offer their respects and pay their tributes for communal harmony.

Baisakhi

Sikh New Year and harvest time for the people of Punjab state in India.

Other Important Festivals

Onam

National festival of Kerala where Christians also take part.

Pongal/Makar Sankranti

Marks the arrival of spring in India and beginning of the harvest season. Also considered as an auspicious day in Indian culture. It is called Pongal in South India.

Krishna Janamashtami

The birthday of Lord Krishna.

Ram Navami

The birthday of Lord Ram.

Maha Shivratri

It literally means the great night of Shiva. This is the day when Lord Shiva got married to Parvati.

Ganesh Chaturthi

Festival and worship of Lord Ganesha.

Hinduism and Buddhism – Differences and Similarities

If you are considering Buddhism as another option then let's take a look at some of the basic differences and similarities. Hinduism is all about understanding the Supersoul or Brahman and attaining moksha by doing good karma, devotion to god and becoming free from the recycle of birth. In Buddhism, it's following a set of rules taught by Buddha that will allow you to become free from sorrows and attain nirvana. Too many, both of these major religions of the world appear the same but there are many differences. But good thing about both these two religions is that anyone can practice them without actually converting from their ancestral religion.

According to Dr S. Radhakrishna - *Buddhism, in its origin at least, is an offshoot of Hinduism*.

Buddhims Vs. Hinduism – Comparison chart

Founder

Buddhism - Siddhartha Gautama.
Hinduism - There is no one founder.

Place of origin

Buddhism - Nepal (Birth of Buddha), lived and preached in India.
Hinduism - India

About

Buddhism - Follow the teachings of Buddha.
Hinduism - Believe in many Gods but form the part of the soul.

Belief in God

Buddhism - Buddha himself kept quite on the existence of God. In Theravada Buddhism there is no God. Buddha is not a God.
Hinduism - There are many Gods but in Hindu philosophers consider Brahman as the Parmatma (Supersoul).

Clergy

Buddhism - Monks and nuns that form the part of the Sangha. Male monks are called Bhikkhus while females are called Bhikkhunis. It is possible to practice without a clergy.
Hinduism - Brahmins called pundits officiate rituals and pujas. There are rishis, yogis and gurus. It is possible to practice Hinduism without a priest.

Religious law

Buddhism - Teachings of Buddha.
Hinduism - Vedas, shastras.

Holy books

Buddhism - The Tripitaka (Pali Canon – the word of Buddha), Mahayana Sutras, Tibetan Book of the Dead.
Hinduism – The Vedas, Upanishads, Bhagavad Gita, Samhitas, Brahmanas, Aranyakas, Puranas.

Goals

Buddhism - Attain Nirvana. Let go of desires, reduce sorrows, ignorance.
Hinduism - Attain Moksha by doing good deeds and devotion to God.

Re-incarnationSame – Both believe in reincarnation.

Meditation and yoga

Buddhism - Mainly Zen Meditation and, Vipassana Meditation.

Hinduism - Meditation or dyana is carried out to become aware of the "self" and become detached from the external world. Samadhi is the experience of state of Brahmana. Jnana Yoga, Bhakti Yoga, Karma Yoga, Raja Yoga, Hatha Yoga – Mainly Patanjali's yoga.

Chants

Buddhism - Chanting of Nam-myoho-renge-kyo to awaken one's Buddha. Types of chanting include sutra, gatha and dharani.

Hinduism - Chanting mantras, the Om, singing bhajans and devotional songs.

Repentance

Buddhism - Practice of repentance by chanting relevant sutra verses and bowing before a Buddha image/idol. Generally repentance is not part of Buddhism.
Hinduism - Concept of "praischit" or repentance is there but one suffers the consequence of their karma.

Attachment to the world

Both believe that attachment to materialist world causes sufferings.

Use of idols

Use of idols and images are commonly used in both religions.

Holy language

Buddhism - Pali, Some Sanskrit (Mahayana Buddhism).
Hinduism - Sanskrit

Main location of followers

Buddhism - Myanmar, Laos, Thailand, Cambodia, China (Tibet) and Sri Lanka.
Hinduism - India, Nepal

Afterlife

Buddhism - Re-incarnated according to deeds (karma). Good karma leads to happiness while bad karma leads to suffering. After liberation, what happens to the soul is not known.

Hinduism - Re-incarnated according to deeds (karma). When soul attains moksha it becomes part of God.

For more information on Buddhism, you can read my book - **_Buddhism Made Easy: Buddhism for Beginners and Busy People_**. *ASIN: B00T73T41M.*

Conversion to Hinduism

The majority of Hindus in the world are born into the religion. They usually grow up in India or another country where Hinduism is the dominant religion and simply get raised on the beliefs found in the Hindu holy books such as the great epics Ramayana and Mahabharata, the Vedas and other scriptures. However, there are some people of other faiths or beliefs who actually want to convert to Hinduism for one reason or another when they are older. You might not think this is a possibility, but it is. In fact, if you live in an environment that promotes democracy and freedom of religion then you can convert to any religion that you want. But just remember that you need to fully understand the religion itself before you make the drastic decision to actually base your entire lifestyle around the principles of its teachings. With Hinduism, there is no exception to this rule. You need to make sure you understand the concepts and the basic principles it outlines for Hindu followers.

Here are a couple of basic points you need to understand. One is that Hindus believe in Dharma, which is the belief that we have duties in which we are all meant to fulfill in our lives. This could be the duty of a specific job or being a parent. The idea is to fulfill this duty to the best of your abilities. Next you need to have full respect for all life on Earth. Hindus believe all life forms are manifestations of God, or the Creator. This is why you have to be willing to be nice and not hurt or kill any of these life forms. You even have to go so far as to respect the planets of the galaxy and sun when it rises in morning. Then if you end up having unsettling thoughts, practice yoga and meditation in order to clear your unwanted thoughts.

Once you have the mindset to become a Hindu, the next step is actually studying under Hindu teachers. Now don't get discouraged because some Hindus may tell you that you have to be born into the religion and cannot convert, especially if you are a Westerner. The reason they say that is because you have likely already committed acts that are against what the Vedas teaches, so there is no going back from that. But do not get discouraged from this because there are Hindu sects that just about anyone willing to become Hindu can go to, even Westerners. The International Society of Krishna Consciousness (ISKCON or simply Hare Krishna Movement) is the most popular sect and it is based right in New York City. Since 1965, they have expanded their centers, rural communities and temples throughout the world. There are even one hundred vegetarian restaurants that are affiliated with them. You can also find local meet-up groups in your town or city that is associated with this sect. Just go to iskcon.org to find one of these groups in your area.

You can talk with other Hindus, go to temples, learn the rituals, and so on. But don't expect some initiation or conversion ceremony where a Hindu priest welcomes you into the religion. In fact, Hinduism doesn't even talk about conversion into the religion. All it says is that you have to let your daily actions, thoughts, beliefs, and way of life be reflective of the Hindu scriptures. The more you follow and embrace the religion, the more you will become a Hindu. Eventually you will feel confident to call yourself a Hindu and that is okay. You don't need to have that title designated to you by some Hindu authority figure. It is a label you can place on yourself simply by understanding the religion and practicing it every day.

What to do in a Hindu Temple

There is more to India than just the Taj Mahal or the forts of Udaipur and eating street food. Lots of people from all over the world of different faiths and nationalities are visiting India to seek spiritual upliftment and in search of inner peace. In fact, tourists from all over the world are visiting India to get to know about Hinduism, the world's oldest religion. So if you are one of these spirituality seekers and travelling to India and considering visiting Hindu temples or yoga retreats then here are some tips that you will find useful. It will be valuable particularly for those who have never been to a Hindu temple before.

So here are my tips when visiting a Hindu temple especially if you are visiting for the first time.

Wear modest clothing

It is highly recommended that you wear modest clothing. If you are wearing jeans and tops, it is absolutely fine, you will not be prevented from entering temples but most Hindu women prefer to wear sarees and salwar kameez when visiting temples. Men usually wear kurta pajamas but again jeans and shirts or t-shirts are absolutely fine.

Cover your head

Although this is not really necessary in most temples in India but some women (and men) prefer to cover their head with their "dupatta". If you aren't wearing the traditional Indian salwaar kameej then there is no need to cover your head.

Don't eat meat a few days before your visit

Many Hindus prefer not to eat meat if they happen to be visiting an important temple particularly if they are going on a pilgrimage to places such as Varanasi or Kumbh Mela. You might consider refraining from eating meat a day or two before going to the temple.

Take a shower before you come

Most Indians usually take a shower before they visit temples. Hindus adore their Gods and Goddess with loving sincerity and therefore prefer to cleanse their bodies before entering the holy sanctuary.

Remove your footwear

If one thing is frowned upon - it is wearing of shoes in temples. Shoes are considered unclean so you will have to take them off. Most temples have free shoe-stalls where you hand over your shoes or sandals which can be collected when you return. It may not be necessary to remove your socks.

Prostrate to the deity

When you enter the temple, fold your hands, prostrate and offer your salutations or "pranaam" to the Gods and Goddesses. Some people touch the ground and then the forehead. It is like offering yourself to God. Always prostrate to the Lord Ganesha, the Elephant god first as he is the remover of all obstacles and he is always prayed to first. All prayers in a Hindu temple start by offering him a prayer at the start.

Sit down with legs folded

In most temples, devotees are expected to sit with their legs folded. Do not sit down with legs pointing to the deities. You can fold your hands and close your eyes. This is the time when you can pray, ask forgiveness or express your desires and wishes to God.

Don't talk during the puja

Ideally, you are not supposed to be talking when the bhajans or devotional songs are being sung. In fact, you are supposed to take part in it. If you don't know the best option is to listen and meditate.

Take the aarti

When a plate of aarti or the "sacramental lamp" is offered to you, you place both hands over it (far enough not to get burnt) and then place it on your head (symbol of purification). The

Gods and Goddesses then bless you through the flame. The light from the lamp is supposed to remove darkness. Put some money in the aarti plate (only if others are doing the same thing). The money will either be taken by the priest or used for temple maintenances whatever the policy maybe of the temple you are visiting.

Take the "Prasad"

If you are offered any offerings (called the prasad) take them with your right hand while placing your left hand beneath it like a cup. The left is considered unclean as it is used mainly for washing the backside.

Remember rituals will differ from one temple to another but these are the basics. Not all Hindus even follow these rules. For instance, I know of Hindus who eat meat and visit temple the same day. That's the great thing about Hinduism; it gives the devotee freedom to think and practice the religion in the manner they choose fit.

If you are further interested in Hinduism or visiting Hindu temples, you might consider buying my ebook called, "Hinduism For Kids". It's mainly designed for children but those visiting India particularly those who will be visiting religious places will also find the book useful. Even if you aren't visiting India but wish to learn about Hinduism then the book will be useful too. The book covers all important aspects of Hinduism and will serve as a beginner's guide to the religion. Another book of mine is in slightly in more detail which you will find useful. It's called "Hinduism Made Easy: Hindu Religion, Philosophy and Concepts". ISBN-10: 1511790172.

Pilgrimage to Varanasi

When I read the Bhagavad-Gita and reflect about how God created this universe everything else seems so superfluous." - Albert Einstein

The city of Varanasi also known as Banaras or Kashi is one of the most ancient cities of the world. Varanasi gets its name from two rivers Varuna and Assi which meet here. Varanasi, a city of learning and knowledge is sacred to Hindus and one of the oldest inhabited places in India.

Banaras, often called the city of temples is situated on the banks of River Ganges in the state of Uttar Pradesh. Banaras is not only the city of temples; it's also the city of lights and the religious capital of India. There is no place in the country as charismatic, vibrant and spiritual as the city of Banaras. The city is visited by more than a million tourists every month. The architecture, colour and noise combined with the spirituality of the place, culture and faith makes Varanasi an absolutely magical city.

The city has religious significance for the people of the Hindu faith and being on the banks of holy Ganges, people flock to Banaras not only from India but from all over the world to bathe in the sacred waters. Nearly 60,000 people take a holy dip in the Ganges in Varanasi every day. Funeral pyres line the river banks (or ghats) and piles of wood and bodies continue to burn day and night. It's believed that those cremated here obtain salvation and freedom from the recycle of birth.

Holy significance of Varanasi

This holy city gets a mention in the oldest of mythological books known to man the "Vedas" along with a mention in the epics, Ramayana and Mahabharata. The city was founded by Lord Shiva and it's believed that if you take a dip in the Ganges, you will wash away all your sins. Although, Banaras is sacred for Hindus, surprisingly a third of Banaras's population is Muslim. Not only Hindus find this place sacred but Buddhists and Jains too consider this place sacred. Gautam Buddha first taught "Dharma" here in Sarnath, about 14 KM from Varanasi. Sarnath is one of the four most important pilgrimages in Buddhism after Bodh Gaya. The seventh Jain Tirthankara (rare spiritual being) Suparshv Nath Ji and twenty third Jain Tirthankar Parshva Nath Ji was born in this city.

A lot of people mostly from the west come here to in search of peace, to seek the meaning of life and attain serenity and inner peace. Varanasi has been a hub of arts, culture and literature. Spiritual leaders such as Mahavira, Buddha and Ramanujan spent a lot of time in this holy city making it even more divine. Indian literary greats such as Kabir, Tulsi Das and Ravi Das also lived in Banaras. Even geniuses like Steve Jobs came here.

At first sight Varanasi makes you feel its aura and one gets to know how sacred cows are and will give you a glimpse of the Hindu religion. There is always a buzz in the city. Of late, it has become noisy, thickly populated, polluted and a lot of traffic. Holy Ganges is no longer pure, it has become so polluted that it has no dissolved oxygen left and has 500 times the toxins above the recommended limit.

Varanasi Ghats (River banks)

There are more than 100 ghats in the city and are used for bathing. There are several bathing ghats as well which are used for cremation. Here are some of the most important ones.

The most popular ghat is **Assi Ghat**. This ghat is most important for baths and has many cafes and hotels.

Dasaswamedh Ghat: The evening aarti/worship takes place on this ghat and forms a spectacular sight.

Harishchandra Ghat: This ghat was built by Raja Harishchandra, a king and a descendant of Lord Rama. He did the last rituals of his son at this ghat.

Manikarnika Ghat: It's the main cremation ghat and one of the oldest ghats in Varanasi.

Narad Ghat: The ghat is named after a hindu sage Narad. It's the only ghat where people don't take a holy dip in the Ganges as it is believed taking a bath on this ghat will lead to fight among relatives and friends. Sage Narad was supposed to be mischief maker.

Scindia Ghat: According to a legend, God of Fire was born here. It has a Shiva temple. Lots of devotees come here to ask God for a son.

Lalita Ghat: This is one of the main ghats of Banaras named after Goddess Lalita. It is close to Manikarnika Ghat.

Maan-Mandir Ghat: Another important one. You will find that the ghat buildings are of Rajput architecture as it was built by Rajput Maharajah Man Singh of Jaipur in 1600.

What to do in Varanasi

Varanasi is a must visit place, whether you are Hindu or not - doesn't matter. You have to visit this place to find yourself a changed person; it's a place that will open your eyes spiritually. Taking a boat ride in the Ganges at the time of sunset is something which has to be done. Also when in

Varanasi, a visit to the Kashi Vishwanath Temple is a must, the temple devoted to Lord Shiva. Jantar Mantar one of the ancient scientific observatories and Alamgir Mosque built by Aurangzeb over the demolished Krishna Temple are some of the other places to visit. This city is one of the few places where government has licensed Bhang (marijuana shops) where one can drink bhang lassies or milkshakes. May sound weird, but you can sit on the ghats and watch burning bodies as the funeral pyres burn constantly - 24 hours a day, 7 days a week, month after month and year after year. The place does not evoke fear and you might even feel the presence of the lord. Photography is not allowed at the cremation grounds but you can take photos from a distance.

Delhi to Varanasi

The best way and the fasted way to get to Varanasi from Delhi is to fly from Indira Gandhi International Airport to Varanasi Airport (also known as Lal Bahadur Shastri Airport) on the numerous Indian domestic airlines which take about an hour. There are plenty of trains from Delhi, mostly overnight. You can check train times and which trains are stopping at Varanasi here http://www.trainenquiry.com/. Although coaches are slower and noisy; travelling to Varanasi by road can be a quite a pleasurable experience.

Having lived in Banaras for many years (my third home after Patna and Delhi), I can say that I loved living there. Although the city is crowded with lots of small by-lanes, lots of beggars, and horrendous traffic; you will find everything you need in this place. Varanasi is also well known for silk weaving and apparels. Banarasi sarees (worn by Indian women) are very popular. If you are one of those metaphysically inclined people, then a visit to this place can have a profoundly peaceful effect on your way of thinking. When you are at the ghats, make sure you take a boat ride and you can always have a guided tour which should cost about 200 to 400 Rupees. Make sure you take a camera with you.

If you want to experience Hinduism in its rawest form then I suggest you visit Banaras at least once. I come from a family of priests and do know a little about Hinduism. So if you wanted more information about Hinduism and considering visiting India on religious tour then don't hesitate to ask me a question here on my website http://www.shalusharma.com.

Hindu Mantras

Mantras are an important part of the Hindu belief system. They are sacred chants that are composed of one word or a group of words that form part of hymns. Most original mantras in Hinduism are in Sanskrit but some are in Hindi and other local languages. Mantras are usually spoken aloud.

Here are some popular mantras for you to chant.

Om (Aum)

This is the most widely used mantas and the simplest. Om is considered as the source of all mantas. You can simply chant Om whenever you like and as many times you want. It's an excellent sound for you to meditate on. Simply sit down cross legged and chant Om.

Gayatri Mantra

Aum bhur bhuva svah, Tat savitur varainyam , Bhargo devasya dhimahi, Dhiyo yo naha prachodayat

The Gayatri Mantra is one of the most revered mantras in Hinduism. The one chanting this mantra and the one listening to it will have their divine self and their soul awakened. It is also thought that if spoken it causes spiritual vibrations and induces powers of righteous and wisdom.

Shiva Mantra

Om Namah Shivaya

Lord Shiva is the God of destruction and part of the trinity of Gods (the other two being Brahma the creator and Vishnu the preserver). Whoever chants this mantra will have their true inner self awakened when chanting his mantra.

OM Tat Sat

OM Tat Sat, OM Tat Sat, OM Tat Sat

This is a very simple mantra which means "the three words of the three forms of God". It means that there is only one God and there is only one truth. It is thought that if you chant this mantra it will liberate you from the recycle of birth.

Hari Om

Hari Om, Hari Om, Hari Om

This is a simple mantra which can be chanted anytime of the day. Many Indians like chanting this mantra while taking the bath. Hari actually means God but in this mantra it is directed to Lord Vishnu.

Hare Krishna Maha Mantra

*Hare Krishna, Hare Krishna, Krishna Krishna, Hare Hare
Hare Rama, Hare Rama, Rama Rama, Hare Hare*

This mantra is called the Maha Mantra or simply the Hare Krishna mantra. It is simply chanting the name of Hari (God) Krishna and Rama. Note that the word "Hare" is the vocative form of Hari.

Om Gum Ganapatayei Namaha

Om Gum Ganapatayei Namaha, Om Gum Ganapatayei Namaha, Om Gum Ganapatayei Namaha

Lord Ganesha is also known as Ganapati and is known as the remover of obstacles. Anytime you feel that you want to achieve anything then chant these words *"Om Gum Ganapatayei Namaha"* and it will awaken the shakti or power of the universe and the vibratory power of your consciousness.

Jai BajrangBali

Jai Bajrang Bali, Jai Bajrang Bali, Jai Bajrang Bali

Bajranbali is Lord Hanuman, the Monkey God. This simple mantra chanted 3 times will help you overcome any type of fear. You are simply chanting ,Hail Lord Hanuman. It's a simple but very effective mantra for eliminating fear from any situation.

Om Sri Durgayei Namaha

Om Sri Durgayei Namaha, Om Sri Durgayei Namaha, Om Sri Durgayei Namaha

Goddess Durga is one of the most adored Goddess in the Hindu religion. This mantra evokes her name and will protect you against any harm.

You can find more Hindu Mantras in this book – "Mantra Healing: Mantras for Long Life, Health, Wealth, Success and Inner Peace". ISBN-10: 1517536707

Thank You

I hope you have enjoyed reading this book. By know you would have got an idea on the important aspects of the Hindu religion. If you have any questions then feel free to send me a message here http://www.shalusharma.com/contact and I will try my best to get back to you. Feel free to subscribe to my newsletter here http://www.shalusharma.com/subscribe. I send occasional newsletters related to India.

I would like to mention that Hinduism does not always equate to spirituality in India. Indians are certainly more spiritual but mind you there have been crimes in the name of religion. The ancient temples of India were carved of stones and took years to complete but nowadays the newly built temples resemble more like shopping malls. Anyway, if you are coming to India to search for the meaning and purpose of your existence then India is certainly for you; spirituality in India is not dead yet. But if you are coming to find spirituality and inner calm but instead you see chaos, frustration, poverty and consumerism then don't get too frustrated. We are an old civilization and a young nation and we are still trying to get over the basic necessities people from the West take for granted namely running water, electricity and sanitation.

Here are some of my other books related to religion that might interest you:
http://www.amazon.com/author/shalusharma

Hinduism For Kids: Beliefs And Practices

Hinduism Made Easy: Hindu Religion, Philosophy and Concepts

Religions of the World for Kids

Buddhism Made Easy: Buddhism for Beginners and Busy People

Mother Teresa of Calcutta: Finding God Helping Others: Life of Mother Teresa

Tao Te Ching: Tao Te Ching of Lao-tzu: Book of the Way

Recommended reading

Here are some interesting books:

Mantra Healing: Mantras for Long Life, Health, Wealth, Success and Inner Peace

Lectures on the Bhagavad Gita (Annotated Edition)

Raja Yoga By Swami Vivekananda

Indian Religions For Kids

The Song Celestial or Bhagavad-Gita (Annotated)

***

Made in the USA
Columbia, SC
20 September 2018